Glass Is Elastic

JON GLOVER was born in Sheffield in 1943 and grew up in south London. He studied English and Philosophy at the University of Leeds, where he met Jon Silkin and began a long association with *Stand* magazine. From 1964 he has helped to produce and edit it, together with Jon Silkin, Ken Smith, Rodney Pybus and Lorna Tracy and is now Managing Editor of *Stand*, working with John Whale and Elaine Glover. Jon Glover is an Honorary Fellow of the English Association, an Honorary Fellow of the School of English at the University of Leeds and holds an honorary doctorate from the University of Bolton, where he is Professor Emeritus of English and Creative Writing. He edited *The Penguin Book of First World War Prose* (1989) with Jon Silkin, and is currently researching the *Stand* and Silkin archives held at the University of Leeds and working on a biography of Jon Silkin and Silkin's *Collected Poems*. Three previous collections of Jon Glover's poetry have been published by Carcanet.

T0099116

Also by Jon Glover from Carcanet Press

Our Photographs
To the Niagara Frontier
Magnetic Resonance Imaging

JON GLOVER

Glass Is Elastic

CARCANET

First published in Great Britain in 2012 by
Carcanet Press Limited
Alliance House
Cross Street
Manchester M2 7AQ

www.carcanet.co.uk

A CIP catalogue record for this book is available from the British Library

ISBN 978 1 84777 114 8

The publisher acknowledges financial assistance from Arts Council England

Typeset by XL Publishing Services, Tiverton
Printed and bound in England by SRP Ltd, Exeter

for
Nancy Shaver and Jackson

Acknowledgements

Some poems from this volume have appeared in the following journals: *PN Review, Stand, Poetry and Audience, Review LISA / LISA* e-journal, vol. VII, no. 3 (Caen, 2009), and in Jemimah Kuhfeld's *The Laurel Crown – a collection of poems and portraits.*

I acknowledge generous interest, advice and friendship from colleagues in the Universities of Bolton and Leeds. Support from Robert Campbell, George Holmes, Sam Johnson and Peter Marsh, in terms of time and finance for research, including writing poetry, is acknowledged with gratitude.

These individuals have been important in reading and discussing these poems: John Barnard, Carole Bromley, Anne Caldwell, Shirley Chew, Mary Cooper, Hannah Copley, Mick Gidley, Phil Isherwood, Janette Jenkins, Evan Jones, Zoe Lambert, Ed Larrissy, Bethany Layne, Grevel Lindop, Owen Lowery, Michael McCarthy, Ian McMillan, Dorothy Nelson, Stella Pye, Amy Ramsay, Sheila Roe, David Rudd, Michael Schmidt, Les Smith, Simon Smith, Julian Turner, Jeffrey Wainwright, John Whale, Pat Winslow, and many recent MA Creative Writing students including Leon Borders, Varney Cooke, Michelle Paramanantham and Anita Parmar. Dr Charles Lee provided an inspirational role in explaining Ancient Greek geometry.

Chris Sheppard, Head of Special Collections in the University of Leeds, has helped to provide a scholarly and creative environment invaluable for the study and writing of poetry. His colleagues, including Kathryn Jenner, have helped in the production of this book and others under way.

Rachel Falconer, Adam Piette and the late Sean Spence of the University of Sheffield helped directly and indirectly with the 'Narcolepsy' poems. The Seamus Heaney Poetry Centre at Queen's University Belfast organised a heartening conference on poetry in the autumn of 2010 which helped this new volume to progress.

The staff of Carcanet Press have offered faith, imagination and efficiency – thanks to Eleanor Crawforth, Michelle Healey, Pam Heaton, Alice Mullen, Okey Nzelu, Stephen Proctor, Michael Schmidt, Christine Steel and Judith Willson.

My wife Elaine has, as ever, encouraged my writing as have Abby and Rhiannon and their husbands and children. Thank you all.

Contents

Note

Hand It On

Counting the birds' wings' most intense beats
for, I guess, one-and-a-half seconds
till they stop and loop downwards for half-
a-second more in silence, it's so

much like taking a photograph as
a way of speaking of what we've seen.
Or hand-and-finger-signing through some
impairment, possibly. If I can

reckon it and time it, that's surely
a composition, the way to make
it an inheritance. Hand it on.
I like that, counting the way the birds fly,

on and in your hands, tapping flight out
as a real token that I can
hear, sorting out simple change from a
new commodity. It can build up

like solid coinage. Instant, handy
as such. Though hard to follow the trick.
Where's that real number behind my skin,
the sounding, clapping game? A sort of

mathematical palmistry.
I can count on those lines and creases
being there. But the other pictures
that slither through are all wings, just gone

immediately. I'm having you on. Stop
it. Feel the prints, so well exposed. If
you know what you see next I wonder
if you'll know yourself. Tap the message

quick, the rhythm of your agile finger-
tips. There, its database past telling.
Just as pressing clean sheets of photo
paper into a dish of hypo

fixed whatever it was, caught in the dark
and the safe-light, fluttering unheard.

Mercator's Projection

1

This natural world. Universal
choices. I sometimes see it as an
exam with historic spectacles:

all these curvatures – of lenses, of
the sea, spreading apart high twin towers.
Leading up and down to bend the truth.

To my way of thinking, or yours, right.
Whatever. Mercator's projection,
like a carefully peeled fresh orange.

It's supposed to be the best for some
purposes. My atlas gives other
versions. They look like bananas or

pears, knifed with care and pictured for the
record. Obsession rather, all this
lovely waste that we live on. Skin, I

see it everywhere, the largest single
organ. Chuck it. Scrape it noisily
off the chopping board. No earthly use.

2

I know that early lens-grinders made
money out of sight in the Netherlands,
Germany and Italy. Think of

their announcements carried abroad on
horseback with samples of new lenses
combined in order. Over the Alps,

across the sea. There's one timetable for
shoeing, one for food and water or
fast; staging posts and ports have their own

authority, though from where I am
it looks like decomposition might
be next. Wait for a new focal length

neat in my fingers like reins. That way
or this. Over the mountains, language
to language, to the highest bidder,

to instantly evaluate what
might be approached absolutely, and
be placed on the map as soon as the

cylinders rest unpacked. Baggage, with
contents precious to whom? For glass so
carefully wrapped and, wonder, disguised

in wood and leather. Slick preserves. I
can't surmise how it was displayed and
tried. So much to lose on the way. Through

customs – it's how it's seen that matters.
Does it sit comfortably, like a
new chair or a knife? Shift. The horizon

comes closer, a ship's mast is so clearly
sinking in the distance in the glass-
blower's liquidity. So how to

spread that on the map, and lay it flat?
Follow some praiseworthy medical
procedure? Fleshed, illuminated,

enlarged, a body's so attractive.
Circulation of the blood discovered.
Waves trapped in so cleverly, behind

the objective. But now it seems so
obvious. Round and round. Grey tubes and
dark red stuff in passages to rot.

Skim the light. What's left without it? Feel
a pulse? I can't say where it started
I don't want to see that much, ever.

National Grid

To my astonishment, I found that the great majority of the men of science to whom I first applied, protested that mental imagery was unknown to them, and they looked on me as fanciful and fantastic in supposing that the words 'mental imagery' really expressed what I believed everybody supposed them to mean.

Sir Francis Galton, 'Statistics of Mental Imagery', *Mind* 5 1880

There are batteries whose positive
and negative contacts are so close
that you can hold them on your tongue to feel
if there is any power left. And

not pain, but savoury, cold metal
jumped to twist at roots I'd never known,
and surface to come clean. It may be
one way to make the imagery

display heady 'illumination,
definition and colouring'.
Let go quick. Untouchable? But with
a sweet and acid taste. So off you go.

What could be put into words went off
round the world. Galton wanted to say what
was in his head. A conscious choice then,
and so still — all applicable. But

what if it feels as though the circuits
are losing power. Plugs too worn, or the
fuse has gone. What resistance in a small
light bulb? A tiny torch seems enough to

slow it all. Power generation, that's
what it all needs. Cross country to go.
I think I learned as homework: chemicals
and voltage were rationed out to keep

us going. Coal fired. So clever and
rational to lead it up the street
to comfort the lot of us. Who would have
thought it? Though cables around the floor

to run electric fires at home said
it better for me than a lab might.
Step over or trip. That's no question
so watch it. There's so much to acquire,

with practice, of memorable raw
materials to be reclassified
from mining into proper workers:
impedance, static, potential,

imperial measures to bring it in.
Mile upon mile of force. I never
noticed the language; such science
of the national grid used for its

instruction, all the metaphors of
colonial power. Pick it up from any
map with the red countries enforceable
and ordered. Boundaries through Africa

were easily ruled through surveyors'
sight-lines. Surely straight. Set it out at
a certain age like the threat of national
service or some hidden atrocity

and it even runs the future. All
the facts to be loved and learned by heart,
or else. Shocking to look back on. Was
this some geographic flux that left

me splitting wires to run another
fire? I recall plaiting bare copper
strands, to make sure they'd hold, and winding
them with insulating tape. Hide the

twists. Pull, to test them clean and safe all
together? Some curious and harsh
imperative wants to know. So close
your eyes and feel; tug, it's only near

underneath and nowhere else. Secure
and humming as the next power cuts timed
in. Get the picture, democratic,
if pitted and grey, dulled in a pale

exposure to cherish in a family
album. It's simple to say it's those
slowed-down nerves. Whose truth? Not mine, I'll wish.
You've got it now. Screw your eyelids tight

shut. Nothing's too much trouble yet, so
repeat it and get it right, fitted
close and warm to link the energy
in a diagram to circulate.

Minute

Think of the spatial representation of time.
W.H. Watson

By the time it's a book
it's all over. Yet, even
so past, it's there
on the page, all
dates and numbers.
Try this, on purpose:
Elizabethan Miniatures
printed in 1943
and revised and
reprinted in 1949.

An odd legacy of
wartime to celebrate
what is 'giuing true
lustur to pearle and
precious stone'.
In peace or faith or
fate it 'worketh the
metals gold or silver
with themselfes'.

And thus, on offer,
an imitation as,
or is, a tiny painting
to glow on rationed
paper. Keepsake.
Edit it, print it,
sell it, look at it,
someone said.
The shining finish
of a goldsmith-painter:
there's not a lie in it.

For ever. Not even as
variable as an x
in algebra. Or the spaces
between frames
in a movie that
make the celluloid's
funny stills flow
without a judder.
Over any screen and out,
I would hope. Right.

Don't Go There

Among places I don't go to: the
village in Dumfries and Galloway
where my mother's ancestors may have
lived. In a book of sermons handed

down from the seventeenth century
'to keep it in the family', as
they might have said when adding one more
signature inside, I can read some

faint and unfamiliar names and dates.
Drive there? To observe, or stand by, law
or faith, or promise or timing. Thus
to keep appointments? And meet? Go on,

think about the person who will hold
it next. Who and where? Is that a real
question? Or a dream, a prediction?
Who's asking? It's a funny way of

writing sex into landscapes, seascapes.
So touching. Who writes on that page in
another hundred years will be far
gone, surely, tracing some figure, or

body, into the coarse-weave old
paper and inking in another
painful birth. Conversion to something
like a map of bits of flesh spread out.

Whithorn

With time and space and to be nowhere
near a small fishing port that records
men who went down as the cabin lights
crashed out and the water tippled in.

Always happens. I wonder at how
I'm pulled to that. One modern instance
of a place becoming truth again
with something personal that others

don't suspect. Can't know. It's odd to think
it might grow up to be a sermon
(not mine, I hope), or a picture in
my head that aches to get out there. They'd

say all my imagination can
permit is crass irrelevance to
those there, before and after. So judged,
although unproven; perhaps worth a

trial again. Even so, such a trip
is nothing like that awful risk, a
form assumed like an inherited
disease with the genes from him or her.

Love or blame – it's obsessive and so
familiar. Too easy to get there.
Go to the dictionary. For page
past page the links sound correct

and tolerable again. Family
trees written out as they go along.
Forget the drowning stuff. It's set on
paper, editions accountable.

Or impression, when pen or typeface
pushes in. Want the guilt? Lodged in a
picture of Whithorn when the trawler
sank? They found the boat. An impersonal

part of speech is all I can offer
them, lifted. Should I see the quay from
where they left? Desire it? Not so much.
What could be so old to sign in or

sign away grammatically? News,
film, and scholarship seem quite enough to
see it all in print for the next lot,
generations.
                    Or to feed a poem
that lets someone's parents loom from the
breakers, and pass on by into some
new current English. Or the machair.

First Impressions and After

The first run of a book – a first impression.
For a second to be ordered it would need
wonderful sales. So, to start again, and hear
ideas, if that's what they are, forms noisily

hitting page after page. Really too quick
to squeeze in a visible pattern as
a head or hand might leave to rest in a
cushion or pillow in bed. But it did.

As if in other languages to sleep
on and then easily erased; just plump
it up. But print is at your finger ends
where quick hot metal was; you could count the

characters and spaces, as if you might
want to, with your eyes closed. It feels like this
touch could be endless. Paper so thick with
stories and numbers goes on. Though it's no

good trying to feel it all. There's too much.
So, don't think of it. Don't push it. After
all, the print can't go on for ever, there
must be a finite number of books and

other sorts of pages. That's no way to
reach some sense of everything being
there, or infinity pressed up, and packed.
But it's tempting to pick at, scab (don't, it'll

scar), a graze, they called it, something in your
hands that loves some solid distance through your
skin as never before. Here's a nice trick
if you want it so badly: there used to

be a curled sign on the outside ring of my
camera lens to be twisted to the top to
bring all that could be out there into the
objective. What a wonderful con. From

Close Up to that, it really had to be,
so believe it. I think I did. So talk
it through, talk it out. Too much stuff crowding
to get through the glass. I don't know what it

was then. What's behind a print-out of all
those formulae? As if they're all over
and crawling through thick transparent jelly
to the retina at the back. Possessed

refraction. Split colours from as much as
anything that could be hoped for. From what?
I'll make it seen; that's where a lasting high
res impression comes from. An infection,

such as sympathy imprinted so it
won't get loose. No way out of what you've got
in your eyeballs. You can see it over
and over again, true. No translation.

Nothing Brighter or More Blank

Another telescope has gone off into space.
That's pleasing. But isn't it weird that no one
will need to sit for hours with eyes pressed
to a cold lens, in stillness, shivering through

the night. Computer screens and digital images:
that's the way to buy the moons of Jupiter or
a lunar sea, all shadows. Frame them for the wall,
print them for a library. Pretty and costly.

How do they do it? And pick up signals
from such a distance? And close up, so gently
with all that fire to lift off. It'll need nothing
to see through or dust or polish. It's gone up.

Our choice, highly taxed, to pick out rays that
can't be seen by us as yet, and spread another
picture out someplace. Stunning. Just the word –
for explosions and the reconstructed colour

filling in for the afterlife, and just to confirm
there's nothing there. What a relief! Gamma rays,
and lots of others. To be displayed and talked
about in words and numbers that will do for now.

Would I take the kids to a gallery of famous
mathematical print-outs? Here's a wonderful
sum that will go on being divided for ever –
but its beginning is here, so take a deep breath,

suck and blow the figures away into the atmosphere.
Coloured space, sure, it's what the artists need.
I think we learned that by heart. Like a parabola,
describing something pathetically wanting. 'Lacking'.

Like that. A sort of paint job might cover it. With a
gesture, a flick of the wrist, something quite invisible
just brushed up for any to look at. Multiply what you die
for again and again. Just follow the rules and you can

count it out in any language. Let's start with a
whole new alphabet. And more. Where you don't
know it, such speech might be lovely to listen to,
so satisfying. Nothing brighter or more blank.

Evidence

1

To place yourself in history; it's not
that complex. It seems we do it readily,
filling in digital boxes for a passport

or credit card. An everyday task both
easy and boring. Place of birth. Date
of birth. Security data clues to un-forget

your password: mother's maiden
name. There you have it, a new screen
wants from me what's become an

unforgettable hint of what small loss
and gain's now tolerably shared as a
given name to be given out as code.

Stick with it. It buys me out from
re-living (don't think about it),
her habits of romance or desperation.

And his, and all the times they
carefully forgot. That name, oddly
digitised as an express route to

someone else's past, prompts my
worth displayed. By identity theft
from the past quite slick. Try stealing

into half-forgotten thrift and rationing,
milk-tokens, boiled bones again
through whatever the barcodes mean.

The password lets me in to somewhere.
Can't see in. It works right round
the world, conjuring you up (choose

who that 'you' may be – yes, you can),
as if this magnetic strip retains
whatever force was there to cast

a role that might change hands.
Marry it. Easy now. Once. And
again. See, you're able to click

banknotes from a hole in the wall.
Such a cheapening power,
though timefree, and there's

no way to pay it back to you
or to any distant namesake or
to see such shock again. Or to

refill, in cooling type, those
blanks from wartimes that
filtered detail out. Diseases,

operations, education, births
and deaths – fill the boxes
and wait to see the facts on paper,

as cash, human additions and
subtractions logged in. Stuck fast,
retained as data. So no way

to love or know; too fantastic,
they didn't say or need to clarify
so now it's theft it's been, for sure.

2

Go all the way back there? Exchange?
Want it? And what could re-living be?
Think of really doing it. Before

antibiotics. Blank, days of pain
that stopped everything. Forget it.
Yes, no way I could buy in to all

those passionate, momentary
wish-lists of, to them, common
and priceless things they must

have wanted to never happen
again. To anyone. Wishes, day long,
night long. Look, don't take.

Think of costing the pain. Deeds
beautifully initialled so there's
no going back. Moving houses,

moving beds, moving sauce-
pans and unopened tins of green
beans and hoarded bags

of sugar. String. And there it goes,
off in a thought bubble.

3

I tried to write about. Try again.
Once, writing in 1976, seemingly
hopeless associations and metaphysics

with a poem that was supposed
to have something to do with
Vietnam, and its place in History

and more local unrest nearby
about work and pay and about
what happened underground

when things started shifting, really,
the seams did, and the retainers
of revenge and justified draft. See

now. What have I done with it?
It was catching a ride then
and it seems it is still, just though

not justly, squeezing our anti-
Vietnam protesting action, and
the striking miners and a very

small underground rock slip
into what was, I fear now,
a hand-me-down bottle

of eraser fluid. Remember that?
Whiteout. So I've hidden
the message again. It's easy

when you've signed up. Which
I did. Service, again. About a
poem, which was the least thing.

4

Not sure if I've got a copy
but I recall the first words were,
'I was born in war'. Bracket them.

Delete or not? So there's a sort
of marker. Go back years
to find such a prompt.

And over and over. Was it
evidence? Jon liked that line
but the rest didn't work.

Politely, to be kind, he wrote
just particular words were wrong,
and the whole time-travelling

enterprise I left as it was.
Not to be. Really there's nothing
left to conjure with or bring to life

with horror, sex or causes safe to
argue with. Untranslatable.
Unrealised stuff. Shut down.

Or, at gravity's thoughtless
restlessness, slipping like heaps
of spillikins dropped for the

children; the whole point
of the game is that it collapses.
So much. So little. And letting

it lie like that is so grown up.
Teach your fingertips, I think
they must be so like children,

their adult roles, with patience.
That'll learn them. It's playtime.
I'd no right of association.

5

What now counts most in your
parents' stories that they left out?
Especially for you. (First or Second

Person will do for now. I'm happy
to leave it open.) What might you
edit in from lists of discoveries

or famine overseas? Which wars
would you choose to find your
parents' birthdays in? Open

the box. Where to fit just causes
of some plausible truths, mementoes
of how you got here? The vacancies

seem too nicely spaced out. A line
near the Great War could be about
right. But twelve years before,

not after. And then the other conflicts
silencing anyone's expectations of
shared talk. 'Shut up, won't you.'

My mother's was two months after
the end of something in South Africa.
Family in it? Or in the next ones?

Left out, or protected? Strikes
and revolutions, all those library
shelves of distant narrative –

Spain, the Second one, Hungary,
Suez – they all went silent.
Which left things as they were.

And as they are, so serious.
I remember them saying that
they'd seen French battleships

anchored off Toulon in 1956.
But, when that came out, I was
thirteen and those invasions

hadn't happened yet, so it was,
too briefly, though partly secret,
a fact left out in the open, invisibly

between the generations. Still,
of course, a new silence hunkered
down. Choose words, choose

pictures, it's impossible
to repeat what you've been given.
From the open silence, I mean,

I've been given. Or not. For what's
left out, outcast, there's not even
a list of clues or names that you

didn't pass on. Electronic links
fix something like a record.
Listen in on the spot to what's

omitted? Still want to? What
would have been betrayed
if you had owned up? History,

intentions, sorrow, your risks,
I think, were confined to private
language. As such, it didn't exist.

With Verbs

It should be so easy to get the words right
for anything. Alter a few letters or sounds
and you've got the past or future. Perfect –
if you will. Here are some of the others
to choose from: what might be visible? I see,

I see across the avenue. Something so quiet
and dull. Leaves half-gone. No green. And,
with no intentions, it's becoming (become
already?) unrealisable. All the fragments dropped,
since yesterday, was it? It's only provisional.

'So autumnal', won't do. Why would that bother?
Baggage from somewhere, conditional. Drifting.
There's no authority for what might happen.
No accounting for tastes. So there. Wet and dry.
That's all. Even the birds are colourless and all

mixed with viruses it seems. Scooping food in flight.
Catching up with romance full-bellied. How do
they know that? Close up. Lick your lips – for a grand
tour and think hard. By flying out and back. What's
got bird flu or insects with blue tongue, contagion

from the sky? Known and. Just lovely through the
window frame, aching to be screwed up like that.
I'll drop the subject. Tenses to be altered. Chucked
or shaped so tight. Hold it an instant, and now you
may touch and have it all. Should you wish.

Cold Gets Inside

1

The cold has come. Fragile, just like any
state of affairs that wants to settle down.

If it's come from some past violence that's
breathing out its last lungful into the quiet

then sponge it over, squeeze it out. Leave it.
Who knows? Though it could have been on

the charts for last year's weather or just present
at some time. Whenever. There went the jet-

stream. There went blocks of air in the dark.
There went ice-sheets. All unseen, and what's

left is slowing down and obviously colourless.
Atmospherics brushing out. Just blown over.

2

The first time one of the grandchildren asked
about my childhood it seemed natural enough.

But the question changed in my head by next day.
How odd to be seen as something so utterly

different from them, to have asked about a world
that must have been as real and unreal as a story.

Bedtime. And all I could think of was the frost
in patterns on my bedroom window, and reaching

up to hold the curtain back and see fresh light
through peacock tails of ice. And all I could

think of to tell them was seen through those
cold feathers. As though even the summers

were snowy and footsteps on a beach were traced
through icicles. An odd comfort. Keep it there.

3

If even then it was changeable – was so. Leave it.
So I liked pressing finger prints into the crystal,

delicate, but springy and painful, as though,
possibly, waiting to stop a glacier just there,

that must be unnamed and unannounced,
pressing its way round the globe and through

that homely glass. Which, though so thin,
stayed quite transparent and unbroken beyond

each dripping spyhole. Flex them; handy. Push,
and again, push. There I was, messing with

the night's pliant decoration, so content
with body-heat that could melt such natural art.

Temperature's displays surely not so frail
before. And then; drawing exercises, so

strangely rehearsing some endless and seasonal
game? Almost motionless by then, even then.

4

It might have been printing itself out
indefinitely, no clocking in or. And, so

unmemorably beaten out; that I'd think
there was nothing left to call up. Even

though this year has yielded back some
familiar loss in the unmuscular slow-down

of a trudging, stolid autumn. Been there.
Some tale again, that could have pitched up,

hiding in a pre-war radio wave with nothing
left at hand to conduct it. Gone universal.

Gone out. It's properly unsaleable. No private
impress waiting, however limited, I fear.

No squashed-in, thick white paper for a
tangible record; or repeating pillow-talk.

5

Headers inaudible. Plucked down insulation,
flight stuff. Shake it out and there you go,

it's flat and unreflecting. But so tempting
and nudging out there. In winter almost

gymnastic. Look. It's taking off all by itself.
Passing by without help. A fiction does

its job, unquestionably loved and relaxed,
and moves on. Lying texts shift for themselves.

All so knowing. Or lying down. So here, they
offer repeat showings, thus, just a little bit

structurally crass, to suck on. Lap it all
together if there's anything left. Tongue it.

Count the beat or visualise it. My fingertips
now feel nothing. Tell it all again, so cool.

Breath

Those butchers' blocks were anarchic.
The very possibility of such thick wood
being hewn and carved and beaten into
evolving hills and dips was beyond

the stock of carpentry or turning or the
repeating patterns of isobars on a weather
chart day after day or contours on a map.
Split bone, split blood, split cells. Fat

so ready to re-tie with string round
a nice joint. And the scraped wood goes
onto the floor. What's to enjoy about
that, I wonder? The leavings of a very

professional dissection swept up and
mopped down. Weighing just enough
for the next day and the next day. Scales
cleaned up as if they need to know how

much they will allow to pass through the
inside of my lungs – that stuff, oxygen,
of course – to keep it all going. Chipping
away and never sure of tomorrow's smell.

Would It Were

Perhaps then the wax is not what I now think it to be…
Descartes, 'Meditation 2'

Stuck with it. Descartes' piece of wax
that he could squeeze and fold between
his fingers. I guess now that the first
time I read that I must have liked it

as a way to some philosophy that he,
at least, could touch – and us? – so I
might too, though 'beeswax' remains
perplexing. Have I got it? Now, I mean?

That immediate feel so subject to the
smell of flowers (he said), its history that
could melt into ideas, to ask nothing back
except that surely it's unchanged. How

would I know if it's too hot to touch?
Think about it. Enough pain there, I
know. So stuff the messages from that
easy connection! Burn them up? Conceive

a flame held close and applied, so wanting,
imaginatively, and its energy
plain hurtful if you aren't careful. Possible,
possible. Press what's left. Into a sight

for sore eyes (as they would be). As when
I said out loud in the car last week, driving
alone, 'And suddenly there were daffodils.'
Or 'are'. Spring, sort of. Say it, it's still in

the present. For now, that tense works. The flowers
are there where they were and are, though I'm off
down the road. The car steers lightly into images.
They're just slipping out between my fingers.

What? Blow them cool and 'Snap!' Some magic, that!
Wow! The pictures fly. Don't breathe in yet, in case.
So, like holding, or having held, a plan to begin
a new disease (such fancy seems), a virus

will do, that's been selected for a state that's
been completely illness-free, mutating
nicely in the sunshine's wreck, but much the same,
with the smell of experimental power.

Re-Hanging the Pictures

Preservation is so risky and precious. Skin, the summer's tan, old leather goods. And drawers of maps that won't unfold. Probably stuck fast on the days we got wet looking for where we were going. Don't ask. And it's all around. Fallen behind the sofa cushions or double-stacked on a bookshelf. Officially to be taught in schools, the knowledge – museums and galleries. Think of it – the Science Museum in London. With interactive rooms, push-button educational relics, the railways, the balance engines and steam boilers hauling onwards to digital perfection. But, locally, where the revolution was always happening, the Steam Museum. It has its ironies. It's close by where we live, half a mile only, but I've never been there till today. What a faff to find.

> A lost surviving warehouse beside a
> supermarket car park. It's surely off
> the map. Mine, at least. Though it's just why
> the terraced houses are where they are. My
>
> 899-year leasehold address might have been
> planned and listed, starting here. I'm screwing
> up my eyes to picture work, but it's gone.
> Who wants to re-live it? I'm staring at
>
> dismantled cranks and cams set out in order
> for someone's solution. Build yet again.
> Slowly back to childhood pain and tests,
> examination through pieces of a puzzle,
>
> IQ for cash. I'm still lost in it all
> though it's well spaced on the floor to revive
> tons of metal engines that drove the cotton
> mills round here. Powered on through by weight,
>
> ropes or leather belts to spin tough thread.
> Looks too nice for all the raw stuffed
> bales from America? Stacked high. To spin.
> It's nice, too nice, to see the outputs of slavery

measured through the internal volume
of each cylinder, piston and flywheel tonnage.
Ounces to hundredweight, it's labelled.
Thirteen tons slowly counting out

and the horsepower, spinning again. Around
and unstoppable like the progress of
social history. Do it or write it. Take it
as it comes. I like the small glass bottles

of oil with dripping pipes drilled into the
tops of moving joints, the rotating links
that shine out. Instead of vocal cords' speech.
And there's a job for you, all day, to fill

clear glass to keep transmission slick. Wouldn't
it be wonderful to see these agencies
of expanding and contracting colony
spaced round in modern concrete mountings?

For clothing. Scrap-yard art, it's still got to be
polished and painted clean into a happy
story-line. New finds wait around for
remaining placements. Fit and captioned. Bricked.

Perhaps, like hanging, or re-hanging, our
pictures at home. You've got to be able
to walk round inside old complex views,
this way, that way. A road or a landscape.

Or trees or birds or households. Inside a
room and on a wall. And wherever that
machine will go. Or run. Up against.
Tack it first. Next. So there's renewed paint

and plaster to stare at. Fresh colours in time.
I can live with this upset visual ancestry.
Displayed better, composed and re-balanced.
Things to be hammered in. Not right yet?

Needs a spirit-level? In glass. Try it. So it's
all in motion but embedded, soft now. All's
art, our love to stretch around in. Pressure.
Vapour. Still. But even a wandering gallery.

Ward Round

Nightingale wards there
may well still be to parade
for choice. A careless oversight,
no doubt. Memory banks
inside fibred with all the new
technology. They're what'll do
for Social History and will
do for us. So thoughtless.

Warfare gets even better
at cleaning, and pulls together
a long view of battle-plumbing.
Staunch. And why get rid of all
that calculated space for nurture,
or nature, that metal caused
and metal may still need?
Explosives' driving force

speaks loads (you can come
on by for cautery or solder),
so just can't let it fizzle out.
Hospitalise the whole lot
together. Whatever the cost,
and however you express
the double-entry book-keeping,
medicine, after the Great War,

surely had many types of
ambiguity. Learning too.
Take it, just take it. Cures or
punishment, it all tasted dreadful.
Retch and see. It's a profession.
Its interests well on, after all, so
pointedly with big hospital-trains
any cure goes travelling.

Operating Lists

Atomic's got the day
with all you need to burn it,
any problem, out. Who's in
along with bugs and breakages
still stupefied? Subjects or
objects, new war's on a progress,
so, worrying about its

grammar is, I think, too nice.
So, Band-Aids for all and you.
In guardians' hands emblazon
which words you shall allow,
yes, 'shall', for you to hold
a permit or prescription
through the old summer days
still waiting and nursed.

Sickening to be counted
and spelled. Spelled out;
there, there. New body-fast
corrections keep on coming in.
School them. Ideally in peace
time shamelessly to name
what you've got so that
if you're not up to carrying

visibly your own keepsakes
others will. For you and us,
dictionary-proud, following
the guns to each ward so proper.
Think 'lining'. As I'm sure we,
I mean 'I', will have it by heart
just sweetly till there come more
nuanced, deadlier languages.

Or Smear

Could there have been any easy way
out? Whatever definitions, it hurts still.
For decades beyond the Armistice
such retributions internalised before
that: Sarajevo, and onwards to the next,

just stuck in hospitals, and homes, as
continuous justification of the whole
coherent dream that bodies should pay.
To someone and on behalf. Who? Know
it. Whom? It's bespoken searing debt.

Or smear. That's painless so far and
perfectly to cushion the parallels it's
non-invasive. Statehood, like longitude
and latitude, spat into a test-tube. So
not like the fatuous flesh-wounds next

door. That'll cost your portion for today.
It saves beating too much love out from
such screaming moral pain. Do cash value
and a maybe diagnosis fulfilled. But would
I wish its hospital record to survive? Plea.

Narcolepsy

Shuffling by burned library shelves
I see odd survivors await some dozy
silence. I wonder at their putting together
stories towards kind formulae for nodding
off. Any reward in narrative scarring?

Or lovely best consumption? Skin's
valued like beaten silver and gold
laid out on food for protection, or
cultured celebration, far away.
Bloody juices maintain. Bomb-

sites and decoration ought to be
disgusting though wanted all the more.
Pant for it quickly and then it comes,
expressively, everyone's dressing-
changes, stoppering the unhealed

hourly, then daily at best, and thick,
syrupy liquor spooned out. Just part
of the same rate of exchange? Press on,
sting's justified, so go on and spread
the word on suffering. Industrial drugs

are right behind you, behind us all.
And just to get through it, or to it, from
my date here I imagine students assisting
in dark awe and quiet, standing to
attention, against the latest bodies. Needs?

Preservations

Funerary blows. As if there could have been
some awful state solemnity in Sheffield's
1920s chemistry labs. That must have been
some party piece to absorb. Like hell with
ceremony. Texts and address slugging it out

for dignity and trash. Got it. Silent stacks
of preservation, glances and fragments
of analysis neatly written up. A new bacterium
(pleased with that identification). Bottled jokes.
I can see right through them without any

precious lingo. Latin for knives and sleep.
Smear again for inspection. Adhered as
pretty bedside wallpaper. Or unrolled and
stuck on cracked window glass to hold the
bomb-blasts out. A nervy, fluorescent

shrapnel eyeful like daisy chains that
you might have cut and pasted for me, mother.
That's some decoration. Shameful. Don't do that
again. Every metaphor's an insult. From here
on in. Though technicians at work, standing

for hours each day round a dissecting
table, must have lived, and spoken, just
a job, ordinarily. Routines established for
post-war flu cases, that pandemic, and,
even stranger encephalitis and narcolepsy.

Glass Squares

Sleep yourself out of the ceremonies still
to come – a good try at speeding up the
next generation's evolutionary deaths and
survivals. Such consent's worthy of much
longer-term research on the whole bloody

human stuff – choosing (really?) to outclass
us all in an ageless stinking path. lab. World-
wide. Help wake them up or ease their way
out? Who's speaking now? Think it through:

adjust whatever drops for experimental dosages,
and section the new day's deaths' spinal cords
to clarify and still each hapless violent impact.
Blah, remains, relics; hardly how their names
will shape, stoned and inserted on a plaque by

the doorway into this place. 'Inscribed.' Why not?
Nerves quick-stained to be visible, and fastened,
(why not risk 'preserved'?), risk, under glass
squares on a glass slide, to be lit from below

and magnified on up through glass. Parts
of my education. Examination's free for
all of us now. What's lost? Pick anything
at home that has no owner. The dead's
possessions will do. Dug out yet again.

Her War Poems

I've a tiny red box, usually hidden away,
from the 30s with an oddly flowery label
bearing, in a far out-of-date typeface, its
invitation to maintain a work in progress:

'1/2 oz. Microscopic Glass Squares. In 7/8
No 2'. Approved to be kept. See to it. For
dutiful growths finely spaced into wordlike
transparencies. Fit for something like an

afterlife. Thus finely, uniquely numbered,
thus assigned airless, brief colourful identity,
thus disposed of. Take a look and pass it on.
So what's in it for me? Hazard: each new

slide a war poem that my mother wrote at work.
But, what a try on. Silently. I fear, yes fear,
such trashy composure. It's another facilitated
death to archive. Booked in. Don't sleep.

Intravenous

The nurse is feeling
for a hidden vein.
There it's got to be.
Miraculous. I'm
humming, for I seem
to need something
harmonious; there
are those sounds you
can't see, just touch.
Some practise to
acquire them as song,
or where pain goes
now. I think of a rocket,
injectors, something
pushing out into a
high air's port. Take
a place in oxygen's
body, it wants it.
A sharp cannula is
nestling in, writing
to warm its bed.
Up in there from
some inside, inwardness.
Hymn's stuff; lifting.
Just think of that:
intravenous journeys
throughout the world
beyond. To feed it,
feed it with praise.
But don't breathe
a word, don't tell a soul.
Who needs pain relief?

1

Leaving NY and then recollecting
the stay. I'm bothered and curious
at wrapping love in this: a last happy
night in Manhattan and then what
might have seemed an easy journey
back to Nancy's house in Brooklyn.

So we wanted to hail a cab rather
than taking the subway and walking.
And a memory of this goes on leaving
(and leading) as it did at the time.
It's only what you saw. As, next day,
we then flew on. Or 'were to fly'
to put it down on paper correctly.

Like spinning, you might have said,
with ease, while crossing Brooklyn
Bridge. Thinking of JFK tomorrow.
Then off into the cool North – no,
lifting through the minus cold up there,
cleanly following, as if being folded
and bound like new cotton fibre,
into the vapour-trail twists from
a flight-slot moments before. All's so.

2

What a yarn someone might have said.
What a joke, you might have said.
Knitting some considerate seadog's
way of speech in there for the record,
like collected folk-songs, trafficked.

So, even for as trade was for sale
For tourists like us in the Sea Port
Museum here, visible from the Bridge
walkway, and tonight from our cab
windows down to the right, as such
used-up past is everywhere, so telling.

3

And such. Not sure what I bought then –
the power of urban starlight seen
from an air-conditioned car? Carry on
across. Beg for it back? It was just
so very composed, moments as if
in history's fabric. The black cab-driver
had Mozart on the radio already
when he said he would drive us to
Adelphi Street below the Brooklyn-
Queens Expressway – few would,
night-time, he said – and he would
drive slow so we could see it all
with music and a trail of cars building
up behind. The night all electric,
and the meter switched off, for my
pleasure, he said, and for ours, really.

And Personal

Desks. To write and file
write and file. Aboard décor.
Ship-bound, homeward-bound.

Captain's nonsense. Nice leather.
I liked a replay the other night
on TV of the Apollo moon-lander

taking off for home. Shipping
of sorts. Pilots and cargoes,
all filmed and waiting to go.

Desks then in a bit of memory,
crystals to get your knees under;
that's some ownership. Over

your lap. Review the polish,
layer upon layer, of stacked
reflections too good to be true,

though from now on such work's
quite unnecessary with all those
invisible gigabytes. Lovely

they are, a billion affectionate
surfaces to call up, a personal call
and close (close out), with

the far side of the moon there
in the patina, at a touch button,
touch screen – just finger it.

Whose print? Naah! Delete
that joke. Not necessary, in space
the link's already cool and done.

Not skinned or stuffed or framed
for the mantelpiece and clocking.
Now, just to be awful and not

be left behind (some matter!),
I think it might need a built-in
atomic itch to make it worth

going back again and again,
and to push for total certainty
up against the wall as décor.
Or as rhetoric so persuasive.

Not That Great Expanding

Reversible adhesion. That's
the way to build the wooden.

Furniture. Listen, furniture
needs the possibility of re-

construction built in. So back
to animal glue. Fat and bone

stinking over the flames.
Or flowers. Set a glue pot

over a vase of jaunty roses.
Picture that now. So it can

come back newly tight.
'Nowt wasted' from slaughter.

And any garden's delicacy
loves blood, fish and bone.

Upside down, I suppose:
a cemetery, a deck, a net of drawn,

dried stuff waiting for purchase
in an odourless bag. Papered over.

Trawled up for all the fast, bright
petals as though nearly scorching,

or getting their own back. Hold it.
So, there's a garden, softly

speaking out a decoration
that's multiplying backwards,

twelve tens, twelve nines, eights,
sevens and then down some, even if
it's an odd way of coming to an end.

Today's Last Site

A castle today, camera ready,
yet another. It's all grey
calculations, at the end of
the day, or, indeed, through

soundly flipped quotations,
something about crows
and woods. Raining; into

a walk past falling stones,
split stone, and, suddenly
the wind, with what precision,
hastens it all. Lovely tomorrow,

I wish. So you might say,
sharply drawing out the geste
from a scan, from new day's

exhaustion, some friable
curtain walls like fiction's
brilliance to begin or end,
passionate. Over neatened

cannon balls, shot guns,
stone windows, oh love,
this was a skill easy to forget

just as we don't re-set a car's
spark-plugs and timing, power
circuits. Swap it all for
electronic distances, living

it out, and living it on, to cook
the books. As, perhaps I willed,
we did, and do, in such

accounted environments.
Buy heritage, buy pictorial
history to kiss. Nearly warm.
Beating pulse. Or clicking

into simplicity in a mobile
phone and talking away so
naturally to someone else

through at least five time zones,
brightly learning it over again
by heart, sweet taste, picked up
composition to defend anything.

Key-Cutting

My cheering prescription
drug has a one-in-a-thousand
chance of granting total
sleeplessness *and* dry eyes,
dry mouth. Yummy. Swallowed
by me, by pilots, soldiers and,
illegally, for 'lifestyle'. And
Academic Study, Exam Revise.
(Correct Caps.) No care-charmer
there predicted. I wonder why
it didn't work for me. Sleep's
still everyday nudging round,
and eyes best closed and
fasting with the world getting
on, whatever. No great temptation
to interfere through sight. It's on
its own right now. Out there
and licensed to kill if need be.
The need's sciences reform
their outputs. Experiments
and trials so hopelessly touching.
Smirk. Nothing will come of it.
I've stopped downing them.
No reason needed or given.
Just to re-form that dry noise
speech. Live it up some more.

Life

To see it on paper as a fountain,
a spray, a mist may be a happy trial
and error. Try them like shoes or clothes in
an open changing room. Remember those
posh shoe-shops with an X-ray machine?
Top of the range for a perfect fit. Waves,
quite harmless, all knew, for looks and comfort
your feet deserve it. Similes exposed:
fashion in science, choice like scatter-guns.
Look at the bones of your right foot splayed out.
Plenty room for growth. That's reassuring
and just as precise as the scale of an
Ordnance Survey map, to shoot it out, save
yourself from drowning in an instant haze.

Chewing Apple

The apple in my hand is musical.
It's a bit tart, he said, the man who picked
it that morning as a gift. Here it is,
something like lemon juice sparkling. Hold on
tight. The boat's rocking with all that noise jaws
force out of my head. Keep chewing. No, it's
inside only. No one else hears, I hope,
outside in world's judgemental mechanics.
If this then that. So much, they like to say,
is clinically proven. What fun that
must be. All fizzing onto the page as
notes to observable data. Ink is
where you want it now, languishing between
your teeth as if the acid's written out.

Inaudible, I Don't Think

1

A post-war airport on the walk to school
in London might have seemed a childhood treat
though hardly part of the future, history.
In another direction were concrete
bunkers, easy to walk to, and marked as
dangerous and secret, to ground-test new
aero-engines. (Must you?) I guess you'd need
lots of steely plugs and solid benches

by the road to parks and Downs, to hide the
screech, not far from choirs and books, and routine,
noisy architectural complaints, all
that reforming normality. Post air-
lift, just cracked fuel-tanks and the stench of drink
passed over, or passed through. Learned war. It's broke.

2

Metal on test till it died carried loud
for miles. Lovable sounds, joining air-raid
siren tests, for all that suburban sprawl
near crowds from London helplessly insane
held for our good. Nice red-brick war-game play-
ground conurbations close to scientists'
thought-through nuclear clean delivery.
Trialling really there new death threats just for

us to register? Who else might listen?
Asylums around. Soundproofed, I wondered?
Run it again. And again till the cold
(you think 'war', no) winter might have released
the engines' duty and all those locks to
save fuel; rationing inaudible pain.

Presentations

Any biography of an aeroplane. Any textbook. Any handbook.
                                                    Any worth.

Any fraction of a chisel. Any love. Any hoverfly. Any fruit.

Any dust of three leaves. Any whim. Any crystallisation. Purely.

Flying in. Brace and. This side of the clouds is still happy.

Even if all alive, but only just so, in a personal history.

The Cutlery Trade

Trash metaphors are where the knowledge is.
Or might be. Think of the villages lost
at the bottom, no, on the sides, of Edwardian
reservoirs. Standing for power. Standing for
industry. Wealth for life as we know it
and the iron age. Cute one. Prompts a query,
sure. Well, from Victoria to recent
hereabouts. That's your answer. If hammer
ponds weren't enough, if drop of old water
hadn't sufficient turning power, if it
had all outgrown the local forge, then build
a new flood. There you are, all the hapless
glory in corporate justice. Open
the book, close the book – all gone, so be off
with you; last turn, for the cutlery trade.

The Optician's Shop Window

1

Look at my eyes. Look to the left,
look to the right. Antiquity is a way
to get there. No, surely not. Just antiques.
A trade that's good enough for exchanging
things of value. So that's how you see it.
Perfect vision. Of what things? What things!

2

All a bit odd to get back there
with thoughtful engineering
like putting your favourite pictures in ·
a wheelchair and pushing them into place.
Closer! Look-it. Look for a comfortable ride.
Perfect vision, again. Oh, the matching
colours, oh, the sight lines, oh,
the perspectives and frames! Push again.

3

So there I was for my first pair
of specs. With the Doctor's Letter,
the choice of NHS kids' frames,
the absolute knowledge
that the next time in school I was
irrevocably in the past. Come for it
birdie, tweet, tweet, you're all
in focus now though still with
allowance for some astigmatism.
That's just a bit crooked. And means
get accustomed. You will. Wing it.

Timing Playtime

1

Second-hand bookshops, spring paint and coffee-
shops, by a nationally celebrated,
so they said, theatre. Niagara-
on-the-Lake is nice, memorably built.
There's the visitor centre with well-thumbed
booklets on near Native-Americans
and true geology, the English, the
War of 1812 recalled and reviewed
in lots of historians' styles from that side
of the river. And all refreshingly twee.
I think it an alternative version
of our cuddly past – choose your destinies
from the ones back home or here – either place.
Fudge and mints, I've souvenirs neatly shelved.
But in my head still a children's playground.

2

It's where we found a parking slot, with a
roundabout that needed a lot of push,
and our daughters loved to see us aboard,
perhaps, a way to divert attention,
or fill in time, from the differences,
the disbeliefs that were unpeeling from
cultural anger, a family plotting
its fall-outs to unlikely perfection.
Timing is all, or was, on the map.
Round and round. Not that such was in anyone's
mind. We'd taken Robert Moses Parkway,
and over the Lewiston Bridge, to see
war's pretty legacies; back through US-
side Native Reservation for cheap gas.

Slide Rule

The shop next door was either noisy, and
sold sweets in tall bottles, or was quiet,
and offered (that word) antique, red carpets.
Capital. A nice clean spend on a dull
Saturday afternoon. What's it worth in
your hand? On the floor, on the wall or well–
embedded in your grey softening teeth? Paid
for. Yesterday's values, hilarious,
waiting to be cleaned and measured – suck them
and see. Sliding fabrics between your teeth
feel smooth and incalculable like the
expensive slow movement of a slide rule,
the best, of course, that offered (got it!) the
nearest clear solution, touched beaten rugs.

Two Childhood Sonnets

Like Beauty

Were you scared? Of the hospital nearby,
of the airport across the road, of the
way that cars turned over, absurdly, in
the middle of the night outside our house?
They were right there, without alternatives,
and even the kitchen drawer full of rags
to mop up the crashed out blood was normal.
Living it out, or, rather, living out
of it, placed anything lovable just
so far away, as the prop-powered homing
planes, above in the dusk, like beauty, turned,
with wing-tip green and red lights, balancing
their helpless passengers' descending glide-
path, to a grass runway. Wakeful; think mad.

There Was Once

A plane's taken up by many others.
A car is parked too close. It's not hated.
A space is joyful. A love rides up and
joins the distance. It's riding by in thought
and is utterly unable to pass
on knee-pressure to canter or gallop
or decide on any moving not pre-
defined. Why bother! Why need? It's circling,
I think, as though it's experimenting
with barometric air pressure or that
extraordinary suction above
the wings that lifts all wings and answers space
back: 'get lost'. But it won't quite yet agree
on its magnetism, its substance slow.

Electric

Coils are to slow electricity down
or speed it up – whichever is truly
memorable. Industrial winding
round cotton-reels or cardboard cores. Wooden
centre-posts scooping up the energy
like candy floss. Mysterious spinning
drums. Voltage is constructed somewhere else.
Think of those crazy words: 'power station'.
Coal-fired, hydro-electric, nuclear
or wind or tide. Song-like imprisonment
for the force that waves along with rolled-up
impulse. I'd like it to be coloured like
reels of thread that spread from spool to tightening
spool in a sewing machine's hidden stress.

Hard Covered

A second-hand bookshop smells. Dead knowledge
is unhappy. Old views are unhappy.
Cast-off cookbooks are unhappy. Dead pee.
I think my fingers are too numb to turn
the pages. Cold today. So likeable.
Bookcases just hold 'em up. I can't be
bothered any more. Rack 'em up. Rack and
pinion. Rail them high up a steep mountain.
All those things that might be perfectly stored
on a pinnacle awaiting a plunge
or a passing cloud or an early gale
from any compass point. But not covered
over by soil or tilth or loam or chalk
or sand or a hard-covered barnacle.

Gardens or Craters

The story of the mental hospital
nearby must depend on who's telling it.
That it was there (large), not why or how, gets
interesting, thinking back. The message
was as clear as the bomb-damage, bricked-up
small spaces we thought then unliveable
in – ever. No one walked the bedroom floor
ten feet up in space. Where? Tangents and sines
and logarithms could fill in the feet
of its sunlit, vacuous sleepiness.
Sobered acres. Sirens. Open Day tunes.
As though, I think now, but really didn't
think then, the vacancies had been transferred
to be cared for in their choice of gardens.

Looking at the Matterhorn, Honestly

Counting out loud
is something to be
learned. Listen to it.

All still happening
as bits of air knock on
through body after body.

Wow, the songs. Know
by heart. Ker chunk, Ker
chunk, Ker chunk. Learn it

now. Just push your head
some more. I'm listening
till it's true, as you might

say of a mortise and
tenon joint. True,
and in line and it's

holding fast. Wouldn't
it be good if the world
fitted with such language

naturally onto itself.
Like hearing the numbers
multiplying for ever

and ever. But starting
here as something for
which you might choose

a punishment or
religion or art form
locked in formaldehyde

or within a wooden O.
And, if you haven't
got it yet, then keep

on trying anything
to get it right. Work,
here is one of my sums

that was right for half
an hour: odd that high
above Zermatt in thin

air and, listen, sub-
zero, the messages
in my nerves worked

better than they had
for years. Did I know
that? What language

was there – snowed in,
glaciated, and
honestly waiting

for correction as my
blood warmed again.
Hear it out slowly.

Snowfall

Will there be snow?
Think of it rolling
in your veins and
arteries like a heap
of white fats and
virus dross down
the road to invisibility.
Pushed. Easy adapt
quick snowballs for
anything that will
make you dread.
You worry, you
hate it. What would
it do for you today
if you got so cold
that you really don't
care or needn't care?

A fair disjunction,
if both reasoned
and carefree, was
something and a place
I was at in 1967. Dated?
Though 'something'
sounds pastiche. (If only.)
Memories adore such
stuff. Sort it. Play it loud
for a show. Roadies.
Playing the freeze.

When I felt the air as
−15° F in the wind
(that's 'minus', not 'dash',
and why not say or write
all of 'Fahrenheit'?)
it was something so cold
I didn't feel. Odd to be
working outside with it

(I did at the screen-print
factory site, physicality).
Or walking in Ithaca,
New York, to some protest
or other. Body politics,
Vietnam in winter.

That was cold enough
for the Northern Lights
to be licking a million
miles across what acts
make body parts of the
universe. Any stretch,
any thickness. Skin it,
just an atom or an
electron or photon
spread to allow it to be
something like the lights'
genitalia (what a word
for that sexy game so far
up there, but no distance).
Touching, so moving.

Though that sky's silent.
Like breath. Or breathing
quietly afterwards for space.
If you could see it passing
in and out of the lungs'
surfaces. Oxygen at play.
Over and over. Looking
back, it's still beyond
belief. Medical warfare.
And someone's desire.

The Road Was

What Nancy said
about my video
follows.
         (It was
some time ago.
Believe it. I'd
never held that
sort of camera
before. What
grammar's there's
a shock to see.
I guess. And, count
luck out, right out,
of what's, several
retrospective replays
on, together.
Verbs disputing
visibly and vanishing,
some hope, blameless.)

She said, or maybe
I remembered it thus
from our Christmas
phone call:
            the road
was part of the house.
You know. And it was
all so flat and I didn't
see that at the time.
And it was green
and luxurious,
almost sub-tropical –
what was outside
the window. But I didn't
know that at the time
you know. Did you see it?
And the sparse, flat house-

interior. So small in winter.
So small and, though
there were no cars often,
and the road went on
flat for ever, I guess
the land went on inviting
me out to leave. We had to.

But I was so glad that
you got the view there
through mother's window.
That was so much. But,
again, you know the person
missing in all this is my father,
so much lost that he
couldn't see or deal with.
What about that. Unseen.
Though the road went
straight into the green,
the rich.
          I'm adding this
I find. Who to apologise
to? The lot of us.
              Did
that rich, unspoken love
practise itself above the
yard-sales, the junk-shops,
and go motoring into
the retail dreams in which
GM punch-press other
worlds (or call them dreams
again, why not, although)
were deafened out before
I could ever ask what
dollars were for beyond?
What were there –
'were there (question)'? No,
'was (statement)' it should be.
Don't question. It's summer
in the video. And nice.

Crops in winter'll work
out enough for keeps.
Unknowable cost. Not
or never there even
if I've bought it so
continuously as a
visual grammar someplace
like semantic jungle
territory hacked out
(don't ask), or a body
on the moon. Or of a body.
By, with or from square
metres: 's what you
pay and pay for. Off road.
Did you see it in the video?
Press *replay* out of choice,
out of punishment, see not.
I wish I'd not.

Icicles

1

Condensing is an old process. Fright.
Or something comes together, all atoms
fill in. Condensation just talking
electronics. Rolling wires. Rolling water.
Raindrops flying their love. Suck it in.

2

Where do you come from?
So many alternative answers
make it stupid. Listen again,
stupid. Repeat after me. That's
where you come from. By rote
which words you learned. And
which words learned you.
Rest. All there back then
in a funny accent, in a funny
chair. And fingering a parasol
already period, antique
and charming. Think of
words hidden from the sun.
So, from the war all around
and nowhere. Learn it, learn it,
learn them. Blank, decoration,
blank, décor in or over the gaps.

3

.I do remember the discovery of
icicles. Break them off
and taste them, bubbles and
grit. What I can't see is
where they were — a window

sill or gutter accessible to
my fingers when I was three.
So there, already puzzling,
a past, a text to drink loudly,
be schlurped in and it's
gone. Through wet gloves
tasteless and heatless.

So easy to write someone
else's poem
on this, like this
like that. As though these
were your very own words
out in the world meeting
an unenviable death
like a wasp in amber.
Angry buzzing, for now,
just leave it alone. Set.

On Adelphi Street

Nancy's house in Brooklyn
was made of wood and
probably kept the cold out
in winter but not the noise
from an elevated section
of the BQE at any time.
These streets, as I remember,
were near the Navy Yard
and built before Whitman
lived in Brooklyn. Leaves
of grass? In summer the
chunky weeds and wild
flowers were anywhere,
so exotic poking through
the junk-food wrappings
and diesel fumes; this
was real urbanity but
so unlike Europe. From
the crooked, short back-
yard pathway, everything
sprouting wildly layered
greens, I could just see
the Twin Towers across
the river. Go tomorrow.
This was all rich enough
with butterflies talking
through their history of
what's mine or theirs.
Just off the plane, through
the Holland Tunnel, through
Manhattan and over the
Bridge it was really worth
the party we had. Mixed up
drinks, water sandwiches
(that's what we wanted
in such unfamiliar heat),
set down (more writing)

in territories with their own
screaming trucks and
ambulances roaring rescue
through humid days and
nights. Not wrong, just there;
just sweat through it, or
remember (rewrite), cold
or feverish, a real consuming
hospitality that rattled past
the windows and through
doors and walls. Could you
dream up such theatrical
curtains, to await applause
no more solid, no more dense?

The End

So unusually sunny.
Why should it be?
Just be careful with it.
Something, perhaps, to
study as part of planetary
sciences, orbital maths,
so real for now in its
surrounding, crying dark.
Up there to look at
through any telescope
with the assumption
that you will look in
perfect stillness. Sit,
don't blink. It's all
moving over and
round and far away
before you even thought.
Or will have thought.
Round about. That's
a comfort. Think of it
as where it's gone.
Geometry should
have filled in the spaces
or dots or solids. Solid's
where you're going, mate.
Right on past the flat
morning's light to where
it comes out true.
Get it right, get it right,
get it right, right, right.
And here's the joke:
it will have been
in the future-perfect
tense and the bulb's
blown neither plausibly
nor implausibly. But
agreeable: kiss, kiss.

Nothing to be illuminated.
Seriously not the stuff.
So just love what you
couldn't do. Go blue,
blurt, bloom out
with the sky in speech
marks printed in perfect
carbon black. Justified,
really I'm impressed.

The War of 1812 Again

Forgotten wars. Perplexing,
just absence. Of importance
and excitement there's none left
around. Charm, like souvenirs
and cheap lead soldiers, hangs out.
In brackets, subsumed, sub-let
and dead as a dull necklace.
A family cesspit. You need
it to bring back any grilled
humourless stink from our own
society's family tree.
It's underneath, you fool, you
can't dig it out. Whatever's
a meltdown, or nearly: Three
Mile Island or Chernobyl,
let's concrete it over. Pre-
cast, quick set. No need for such
calculations again. Just
listen for the water table
under that weight. Hear it coming
through? I doubt it. I've simply
agreed to walk in prettily
redeemed battlefields. Where we
loved. A sensuous day out in
the past. Sum it up. Priceless
shot slugs. Think in a slimy
parabola curving right
across the Niagara
river. Touch up gun-barrel
elevation. Got to finger.
Blot up the formula and
pull it to obliterate.

Solder

The Large Hadron Collider
near Geneva is going again.
Relief to lots of people
(and banks, probably,
and their leaders) circulating.
Last year's search for the god
particle went wrong because
of some faulty soldering. So
much tricky lust and so much
iron. And it's said it's important
for all to understand that
it was the engineering that
was flawed not the science.
That's what the Chief Scientist
said. Funny to think of it
happening right now just
outside the city where Calvin's
salvation might, or might not,
have been predictable. And
for anyone else, how frightening
and wonderful. Live it around.
If they once knew their choice,
that it would all meet up, then
they could do no wrong for certain.
Crash. Finished, known and sorted
as you might do a sum with sex
or food or air or clothing or space
and the 'equals sign', as always
in an equation, would carry what
you know and all you needed
to know. Not that you could see
'equals'. Something to flee from,
perhaps. I'm not at all sure that
I want anything such. I wonder
if someone used too much flux.
Or too little. It's a long time
since I bought any of that

in a tin from a hardware store.
Leave it for the time being
where it belongs, in a dictionary.
Invisible lessons of desire
keep on coming. Feel them.

It's a wood-burning stove.
Drop fuel in. Logs'll find
a place whatever the space
down there on the lower
sticks and embers. Fire and
smoke-stacks. Who cares
for transformation? It's
cold, very. Breathe on. Care
for the bark, care for the sap.
It happens. If you hear spitting,
don't worry. Close the door,
close the stove lid. A signal.
It's all going on in there
with air and heat roaring up.
It's worth watching, speechless,
through the furnace glass.
This is your entertainment.
Think of the planned invasion
from 3,000 miles – it shows some
pitch for delayed gratification.
It must have been bright. It's
intelligent to have set it going
from way overseas. Picture it.
Chess or drafts or cooking pots
all wait turns and turn about
with naval wars on the
Great Lakes, watery creations
sailing by to paradise (small
'p' – it wasn't there, so
who's worried?). Plantations,
Christmas trees, floating straw
and rubber and plastic tubes
over the Falls from sewage
waste outflow pipes roll up
on the shore down here. And
all drying out among fish-bones,
weed and gear for fun that

went in the bathroom last night.
Reproduction and cleanliness
washed ashore with history.
Battle through that for a good
swim. Clean up. You could feel
so much better to know it skin
to skin. Just drop by whenever
you want. The door's right open.

Imagine a creek on the side,
nicely cleaned up with linked
pools and tiny cataracts
to sit in and laugh. Why? Oh,
think where the water round
my feet will be going, down

a mile or so further. With the
flow, so funny. What a diversion
just above the electric plant
downstream. Let's talk about
it on the shore. Explain for
the drama or the politics?

Hardly worth it for anyone.
Or for anything more personal?
No one's history counts
in the here and now. Bathing
is lovely. The water is warm.
Draining a continent's old sense

and giving violence back as a
soft drink. Explicit and evident:
jump to it. It's not sparkling. Old
sciences – what could they do,
so far down the track? Just
going to war or going to school.

I'm worried about what's handed
down when it's already become
an oral tradition. Seems suspect.
Though what stands out, and,
recalled before I'd even seen it,
might just be customary, speech

and all. But is it? No, don't like
that. Textbook story or rumour –
OK in a library. But walking
around the grass of a listed site
all, one might say, signed up,
it's workable. Love it? What's

audible, and might come fluently
later, what's said out loud – that's
beautiful where the rocks fall
down and great chunks of ice
fill up in winter. It's hot summer
now. Reminders of the unwritten.

Try the forest nearby. Try the
Lake District's liquids before the
poets got there in your head.
Too soft? Try the one surviving
Yorkshire drift-mine, with soot
by the mouthful and coal,

and so close to the danger, the
warm, sickly taste of water
dropping from the Falls. Un-
textual, unlettered. What can't
be hot off the press. It's tasty.
So why did we pay the big

entrance fee for all of us,
and study hard the road map
to get here? Spit it out. Though
think again about what you
might be swallowing anyway.
We're in an industrialised

landscape with free well-
marked viewing positions,
free parking, free knowledge.
The enzymes of holidays
and manufacture washed
inwards digest it, perhaps.

Gateways

1

Not chosen to pass the time.
They happen, the regular 'Queue
Warning' screens flash up and over.
This side of the barrier; that

far side of the barrier. Slowing
down now. Get comfy to wait
for an hour. Someone ahead
might have seen the windscreen

very close. It's only so thin, so clear.
Motorway, Thruway speed limits
count for little, counting out.

2

Last week at the doctor's surgery
I stared for, it seemed hours, at an
explanatory science poster
on the waiting room wall

explaining, with multi-coloured
illustrations, the cushions
between our vertebrae. Like jam
doughnuts – engineers' simile

(for the poster was prepared by
a University Engineering
Department). Instructive
drawings, drawing pins, Blu-Tack

off road. When impacted they burst,
and, if crushed, they'll need to be
re-built with plastics and metal.
If, of course. Cartilage and discs –

somehow sounding not so sweet and
edible now, or at any
other time, I hope. Passages.

3

On the way to work and in the dark
coming home I pass the same Victorian,
triumphant-seeming, park gates and the
cemetery entrance. Last night late,

and both sets of wrought-iron gates
well-locked, I assume. Accommodating,
for no reason except, I think,
late again, for the auto-accusation

of something voyeuristic. Everyday
crazy. Lists, lists, odd rehearsals,
and count them all in silence before.

4

The next jam, the next traffic lights.
This is England so they aren't
called stop lights. And they don't
hang from cables across the junction.

Stop signs. Either country, either way.
An off-hand diversion takes me
back to another place. Try
the stone pillars that hold

gateways: for best designs, best
architecture for dour memorials
or pleasure ground landscapes.
The Victorians could afford

that (if not clean water for all),
pay for long-lasting classical
cast-iron, wrought-iron, and steam-powered,
mathematically shaped stonework,

polished patterns from underground.
Try granite, fine text. Try white
marble imports like dried-out bone.

5

Well, as someone might think,
when re-attaching fragments round
a spinal cord, there is a lot to pass
through that hollow and all such

natural passageways. Quarried out
for some fateful nerve-endings to
lie down in. And now, I wonder if
they were then so wrong, morally

wrong, to decorate so seriously
their parks of playtime and
funerals. Perhaps the choice of
rock colours, red, white and

whatever, praised our moves –
then was so well prepared to lock
them up. Till wars re-use the iron.

Dr Johnson Out and About

1

Close your eyes and keep
things turning in your head.
Machines for spinning,
wheels, jennies, tops.
The variants offer obsession.
Or, with thumb and first
finger twist and place the central
balance of whatever you've chosen.
There it goes, gyrating for fun
with its own focus or force.
Or thread or plait or wool
or cotton. Gravity's hair.
Combed magnetic force
round the earth's lovely face.

Shape it. The schematic vernacular
culture or science of a barber-
surgeon. Count the angles
of a broken bone, the shades
of an angry throat red and
bloated just as the accounts
go crazy without double entry.
Some weight of blood.

2

One thinks of Samuel Johnson's
visit to the Hebrides as a nice mixture
of poetry, science and entertainment –
a registration of just what the non-
city world can do in its own languages
of experiment. They've their own
home-based talk, you see. Where
to place a dictionary on top of land

with swelling rivers that stop any
atlas or diagram or plot. Flop thought
down on it. Squelch. Tread out
any definition. Pace and touch.
Just as, at the end of his life,
he stabbed himself to let his
body's excess fluid out. There's
the geography of drainage and
aquatic sport for you. And a miracle
for the economy of print culture.
Articulate flowing lead, like blood, keeps
maps and paper lettering spinning out
for masses of other people, if less painfully?
And you: try for it, like alive in company?

Touring

Touring is perhaps
like learning from
or imitating royalty.
All those, the admired,
with freedom, money,
and burdens, duties,
diseases yet uncosted,

or innocent. Keats got
this far north to Staffa
well before parting for
Rome and warmer air.
So where for me the
learned souvenirs?
No sea-sickness

to recall. But duties
(read taxes or blood),
and the rest to come
as written, prescribed
with what might have
become his job (read
'endings', 'dissection'

or 'loves'). Joined up
as for all. Step on it.
So pragmatic to list
what just impinged.
So touched. Why tot
them up for anyone as
curiosities? Rocks,

chipped fragments set
in silver or spilled
into transparency
in an antiqued frame,
sold for so much,
or so little, as legendary
bluffing embedded

beautifully? In water-
colours drying out.
Takeaway arts, ground
up earthenware ringing
in my head, pigmented.
Let them be so I can't
claim that I'm being

mystical. No visions
in flesh alone (or ashore,
choose, it's free) all
day and easily assigned
to shapelessness. Yes
please. It's what anyone
might well rewrite as

being capable of nothing.
Tough to care for any
sickly landscape visit.
Depersonalise it, really?
So, I'm still drawn
to the island myself.
And for why? Fright.

Getting to Staffa

Getting to Staffa
and that cave for me
was perfect, as you
might say, for some sort
of resolution or
solution. We had done
the trip around the island
thirty years ago.
No landing. But this time
the swell permitted.
An awkward step out
from the still-unsettled
boat to a cold, volcanic
pattern-book, each column-
top a different shape
despite the postcards'
patterns, and one uneven
stepping-stone to another
all the way to the cave.

What fascination,
what noise, what absurd
invited danger as the
swell crashed in with an
absurd, out-breaking
tongue-stroke. All curves,
all close-by watery
thunder-strokes.
'Don't go further.
Don't go past there.'
Well, where to stop
further? Pretty tunes,
fairy tales, geological
time-tables are all
published as a record
of what had been seen,
touched and heard

perforce like orders
from the past.

All odd narrative
necessities, as it were,
to get your own back;
to have it all again
and repeated on
the printed page
as compensation for
what's inaudibly
inaudible. Keats,
Queen Victoria and
Jules Verne memorialised
things. Nice ones. Since,
the regular tourist boats
offer, no, create writing
almost, I fear, to a formula.
Royal, state-owned risks.
Try framing the
aesthetic hole from
any angle. But, hey,
my digital camera
has run out of battery.
So there it is again,
thank goodness; another
way to consign another
visit to the past.
The pixels shelved
in perpetuity.
What a will. Mega
dot-points gone for ever
to just give away.

Steam Engines

Gone down, always
down, as if to glide
underground and slide
by pistons and rods
into life. Engines love
attraction. And to
mine coal for Watt and
become a Puffing Billy
to replace horse-drawn
colliery haulage,
for example, and
was surely nowhere
else to be seen or heard
before. Press on. And
after come slick transports
to any old underworld.
Honest, this has gone
too, though fun at the
time.
       I once paddled
with a group of tourists
along or through or in
the river Styx towards
the cave from which
the guide said it flowed.
'Towards'. It was cold
and welcome on a hot
day's sightseeing.
Safely drinkable
from its many side-springs
dropping out from the rock.
It pulsed on my hands
as though it had thickness.
Dense, mass.
           Word-power,
unpatented slush,
or call it energy

or the numbered laws
of thermodynamics,
or what I've just chosen
in treading on water,
like present history,
ancient or future,
between my toes or
squeezed in my hands
and leaky fingers into
succulent transformation.
So pure from the years.
Hold it there – for a
picture, a completed
thirst quenched, over and
out. Gone is it? Clean
and perhaps only
preserved in thought or
your (my) own dying
museum of antiquities.
Or an album of steam-
train tickets. Or pressed
flowers. Cemeteries
of extinct imagined
forms already happy.

Back Story

Windows in ships and windows
in airplanes are so important,
though the engineering's difficult

they say. Just there so you know
you can't leave early. Just to
keep you waiting. Splash. Stars.

Fright at the cosmos passing.
Phew... And all that's there
might function as reflections do

in the crisp back wing-cases
of today's stag beetle and
yesterday's perfect blue dragon-

fly wings in the sun. There's summer
childhood for now or the past.
Hull down below the cargo line.

And all that weight stuck well inside
as a centre of gravity beyond caring,
as any outside-stuff passes smooth

beside the glass. Polish anything
that's left visible on the inside
if you can. Drink me. Spray me.

And follow, no, recall your transit
through trite airport signage, and
airside security-approved and sealed

pharmaceuticals containers: bottles
to see through to happiness. For me,
for you, quick potions for easing

through space and time to avoid
another boring back story. Cheap
souvenirs of transmission. Futures
needn't be bothered. Look out.

Gardening

If a garden needed
no tending. If the roses
dead-headed themselves.
If the window sill would

clear itself of flies
upturned without
question. If a deep
breath were to be

uncountable or free,
though uncomfortable
but only briefly, or the
journey of gases,

light and necessary,
through what must be
skin-like lung-surfaces
to become a chemical in

liquid that circulates, ker
thump, ker thump,
ker thump and be
counted out as memory

left in dark matter
or string theory
or the other sides
of this atom or that

and was only ever
a nice picture or cute
framework or map
or laboratory to walk in

and talk, talk, talk till it's
all superseded: then
textbooks and formulae
to memorise could be

chucked. And any hopes
or attempts to know
the past or love could
go out the window,

flying till they stop
falling for ever. Texts
(I wrote you then)
passing by and on,

their once easy marks
flop to get shelved
in some other body.
And, what then, if only

the letters could follow,
in silence and breathless
as becoming (politely
dressed and attractive)

sub-atomic implants
that know the form,
would I want it so
drawn out, if only?

Macular Degeneration

So, new but, inevitably,
the star hasn't happened
yet though it's waiting,
three hundred times

bigger than our sun.
Or, adjusting its illumination
to shine up peacock feathers
in expansion, click, click, in a

park up the road. Go for it.
Don't blink. Nobody's
looking, nobody's seeing.
It would be a reward in

a dark corner if it could.
Light's incremental fear
is waiting to take over.
The scores go drifting up.

Do, in your head, the maths
of macular degeneration,
and billions of years come
together. Infra/ultra/fine

pre-chiasmal pics back
up inside. Rule off light's
speed. Years of such big
stars queuing up to be

archived. So quiet in here.
The space telescope that
picked it out will have no
power soon. Blot up the

little creatures of ecstasy.
It was lovely for seconds.

If and Only If

Celebrations cut up, or cut in,
love it all. Praise the choices or lovely
things because you'll need them well in practice
for next year and the year after, if. It's
still a crucial relationship in
formal logic: if and only if –
what a way to pitch your possibilities
into some outer darkness (what a fraud,
what a try on – out, out, out of what
drunkenly shameless window or curtain
or black hole that might be where all minus
sums can kiss and snuggle), like some focal
point or blast yet unimagined. Priceless.
Is it well over there? Just now or
tomorrow in motion? Getting there
quite correctly it could be worth feeling
quite breathless, finely chopping ecstasy
into numbers. Breathe in and out. Done it.
What precedent might you cite for such
jollity? Trouble, I think, get to the library
quick time. All the reference books and
almanacs for tides and suchlike lapping
it up, compose those birthdays on to 20
43 and on. Can't like the sound of it.

Theorem

Lest it happen; and if it did or. Then,
by the fact that it's come out right again,
we, or you, or even I, seem allowed
to take some joy, although it was the words
that stupendously got there by themselves.
Heroic! Voices, palms clunk aloud to

applaud. (Crappy writing, sure. 'Might' should be
in there somewhere for safe keeping.) Check to
keep it vague by adjusting what verbs can
do in tense or mood or person or being
reflex, if there were ever to be such.
(Back off. I might be told off.) That's so old.

Playing language games won't let you off the
hook. (Or, why not?) Prove it all day. Primal.
Primitive – 's mine. Waiting, I think or know,
for the past to be there. (Come back then. Spit,
don't tell.) Out it comes. 've I missed the wordy
shapes of consumption such as rats' teeth, gut

or intestines, bendy white skeletons,
claws? (Don't see what's before you, chew what's left.
Yummy.) Prove it backwards. Rough triangles
Pythagoras proved in your left eyeball.
(Wishbones. Pull and twist to snap the angle.)
Or planted, crabwise, just to squeeze sight's own

territorial imperative. (Love
the proof) that I can see there but they can't. (Them.)
It's all possible. Someone saw the wars
that way, arithmetically correct,
with crowds of smart language operators
that enable multiplication and

deduction way back and further to dust.
Sunlit floating motes discoverable.
Points on a plane or line waste away.
A way to be thoughtless, to have been thought.
It's so calming to set it out. So calm.
No parentheses at the end there. Right?

A Narrative

A narrative makes a dream
very possible. It's the words,
without diagrams or constructions
or drawings of what divides
this from that – so, all those
heroic, failed lusts and the
mirror-coloured flesh that
isn't, or aren't, where the
children got lost again in
another war that was next
door between old battleships
and shelving and wardrobes
with five bent hangers that
smelled of lavender and the
afterlife and last generation's
hair – it's words and dictionaries
that list any perfect right-angles
that must be able to roll unseen
down the outside of the box,
unseeing, like fluff behind the
carpet from the last century,
or dancing like breath into the
next century's hollow and
echoing calculator. So, given
as worthwhile solids aching
through Platonic walls, shapely
and eternal. Or sticky and
uncalled for, last, the very
last short story, with its
ending got to come. Tell tale.

In the Late

On Sundays, in the late
autumn, in Italian towns
the people wear black.

Although it's hot and sunny,
although, as we pay to enter
the Cathedral (the passing

funeral group should surely
have been from yesterday
or the day before), although

inside, there are paintings of
naked flesh (women and men)
being apparently sucked

out or expelled from the
solid earth, and (they) are there
to be amazing or adored,

as you wish, or ridiculed, as
we might ourselves laugh out loud
today at the sights of ourselves

unclothed and without our own
well-chosen protections that
mock and display such wealth

we'd rather not acknowledge.
Fashion resurrected as
witnessed. Pay for it again.

Blue and green striped shirts.
Oh the taste! And happy elastic,
tight but gentle – for the parade

for whom? In shape for all,
worshipping as a stand-in
for muscles that don't work.

Paint over, weave it, plague them,
broadcast it over or under
the usual wavelength or priceless

pink or one gut string vibrating,
or well-fitted sock rolling down
your ankle and off somewhere

else like a tangent that touched
but only just (just say it, it
can't really touch), but even so,

it's left behind something
that is utterly bare, even
of love or belonging or

ruefulness each colour might
have felt as all the spectra re-
converge into vacant white light.

Today

How is it? Why ask? I'm in Italy
and along the road are signposts to some
place Etruscan or otherwise ancient.
What strain. What an effort of attention.
It could be packed in a truck going past.

Goods. Like blood-pressure records – clearly good
for nothing. Or invoice for a gunshot
crack. Yes, heard it, still cost me some. Or all
of us. Listen, and again, listen. In
ancient (good word) and modern in the trees,

below the tree-line. There – bang. All culture's
signposted well towards the uncanny.
Send us the bill. It's dreadful lettering
and figures too large to read. I'll say it's
round the edge and over the paper on

the reverse. I like that holiday as
much as the others on the back side of
a battlefield with the whole stylish thing
in reverse lettering behind glass like
the absurdity of a horse-drawn show

funeral. Days out, days in, of layered
jelly and fruit in an ice-cream sundae
glass. Sugary cold consumption trotting
by; I love it sliced to stand for a new
rifle sightline, taste electrically.

Tangent

Talk about a knife-edge or any way
to a self-sealing surface in autumn
of the sort where the leaf falls off. Circles
and anything that's perfectly disjointed,
complete scabby evolution. Sap, the
bad smell of it's not like compost. Futures –
splitting hairs so it might be. To pass by –
I like it, time's up and near, ever so
near, but just a gone year round the sunlight's
touch that cannot really be. Think of any
such thing, pickled in brine for consumption
a year away. So autumnal with tons
of vegetation falling off – parting
company, bliss it might be. Slicing the
atomic pathways to what I know's still
invisible – stems come on in, or stay
outside. Who cares (question, or otherwise).
Talk of anything looking precious like
a catalogue of kitchen utensils,
I mean, seasonal regrets and pretty
gifts so stainless stacked up through the letter-
box. Old stuff. Cellular reminders floored.
(That's from fighting, I guess.) Leave, or let it.

The Car Rolls Over and Out

Think of a story poem,
embossed like self-addressed,
home-notepaper on a landscape
of clean assumptions and
concepts. Think of assuming
and conceiving all in the
plain blue. Of two metal plates
with your address cast and
squeezing the riot of paper
trees and grasses into hot love,
into a message awaiting
'and' or 'draft' or 'archive'
or whatever might slide past
the car window as it might
topple over down the grass
embankment by an awful
mistake I mean, just see
the grass slither past for
one half or quarter second
as the interaction for good
of a tangent and circle might
do on its way down hill.
That's what I said. It's what
might be narrative of where
plane figures live pressed
into filmic surfaces of
another world. Or storyboard:
Call it saintly for the sake
of the accounts through the cracking
windows (not™) only,
and in a properly saved
and printed copy for filing.

Euclid

What a revelation:
that the Ancient Greeks
did geometry by narration.
No rulers, compasses or
protractors. All that
made sense was in the
story of one shape leaving
and becoming another.
And? Or? Where? 'About.'
How seductive that words
can suck on new squares
and curves like barnacles.
Underneath, can you
imagine what's there?
You aren't supposed to.
Juicy planking, hull down.
You aren't supposed
to see it. Or taste it.
Call it a ship of death.
Around the world in.
It's got to have you
somewhere else. Since
it's to be quiet, so quiet.
And the plot-line is
all that's left. See it
blast off. 'Awesome'
is too cheap to be
about anything.

Divide the Years Down to Seconds

Led (or 'Lead') across
the railway track with
a railway guard offering
his arm (curious that some
know to form that 'want help?'
arm gesture and some don't,
though for years I've claimed
not to recognise the offer),
and we pushed clumsily
a folded-up wheelchair
(the disabled lift
didn't work – joke –
so that's why we all
crossed the rails). And what
I was thinking about
as this happened, and after,
is the attractions of the
word 'premise' (or 'premiss') –
why it is so alluring
or rude (as in 'mechanicals') –
the primitive, almost
stationary, first grey
shaping in the closet before
the words can go out anew,
decently clothed. It's quite
sure, quite safe that the premises
are soft and sweet and taste
of lemon, if anything,
and there they are, though
as perfectly shaped as
a straight line, going,
or a point, though invisible,
and they tell you what they have
just done and why, and are
doing in the remaining
seconds, using all those
Mesopotamian markers,

minutes and hours, by
the railroad track. Possible
somewhere. So now, on
the right side of the right
platform we can be,
as on some stage and
no fright or worries, waiting
by the solid steel, with an
electronic timetable
displayed just above us.
And the next future tricks
and journey times ready
listed and accounted out
in gigabytes, so re-
assuring are the distances
either way. Going fast or slow,
it seems I won't choose from
a map. There was and is
weighty info pulling
across the winter light
like a hefty roller blind.
Or. Rolling ends, destinations
for the years to go. Consume,
packed 'to go', take away ,
take your time. Takeaway.

Glass Is Elastic

A spring returning to place.
A watch, tick-tock, a piston
or gear-lever or choicest

diamond slicing up its light –
all just doing what they are
supposed to do, I guess, so

as a heart returns to stop
and those extraordinary
valves in the veins on the backs

of your hands become immobile.
Atomic clocks – they're all over,
but, I suppose, for all we

use them (for whatever –
medicine or war), they're simply
behaving themselves and keeping

quiet about it. Split the difference
between knowing and not knowing –
oh, the sound of music doing

the maths from guilt, and pain,
alas, nestling in there from early.

Generosity

In an art gallery built
into a lovely (that is 'well-
restored'), Renaissance palace
in a cool Umbrian hill-top

town, I rolled in my wheelchair
(first time for that, there has
to be such an event, I guess),
past intense blues and reds

that listed and illuminated
deaths, and the ways of death,
and many ways of coming
to life. As in a smoothed-out farm

or conservatory; flowery also.
Odour-free, I think. Touch me,
touch me not. All petals that
end it all, and edges of flesh

to celebrate. And angels' wings,
so curiously attached, as though
to seal up a way to the heights –
to look down on all this. Belong

there or not, the feathers have
it all – think of the muscle-power
down your back and the boredom
and pity whilst hovering over

the muck. I think of my wheels
hardly touching the floor in
an ideal geometrical life –
so like floating in the blue

or over the blue in a quiet
bloodless transmission through
the oil paint and out again
except only allowed in that

perfect angle, or in fiction,
that must, just must, destroy itself,
no, make itself irrelevant,
with a happy infinity-sign

bubbling on a shop-window fountain,
or a top spinning its defiance,
or its weight to be expressed
beyond regret. Don't cry now.

Shining

A plane surface is just asking for it.
Would it be the earth or the Earth?
Choose it forever. Over it all, yes,

well-spaced contours or isobars
explaining the weather and the views.
Just there for home satellite tracking

for collared birds, ringed birds,
caught and released like a virus –
got you! Marked on the computer screen

in some combination of pluses
and minuses that must have known more
than I did, or anyone. Digital

adoration that's flattened it into
comprehension – lessons: plane it, saw it,
chisel it – the wood smells differently

with each form of cut. Wets itself. Sand-
paper – listen to it: its name, its grades,
its textures. Its purpose is well-written.

Think of what gets gauged out like a sonnet,
like oil drilling, like an empty waiting
landfill site. Dross, wood-dust, sawdust and all

is ready to float up and away. Motes
in the moonshine traceable fairly past
all your shining eyes. When did you see them?

Forsythia

Textbook stuff – Latin names, parents for
plunder, empires galore. Names from the
first who claimed to spot a plant alive

in situ, grow it home in glory.
Ready freight? For you, my dear, surely
brighter this year. Worthy forsythia's

out again. Glue, the boiled bones that stick
our seasons. Fast, they go. More flummoxed
roaring gas under the glue pot, bright

yellow fright without a glance to burrow
in the glow. Winter's end. Noise and bubbly,
sad dying gold just a few atomic

structures distant from state-of-the-art
decomposition. It's lovable
through any window – you can see the

shapes but not touch. Years have gone by. Whizz.
And spring next, adhesion made of waste
bits, though no old tendons pull towards

next year. Stew this for someone else's
holier battle. Wave now! Off they go.
The seasonal liquid's set fair. What

offerings! What would it smell like next?
Slaughterhouse droppings for sweet old dry
summertime. Join, join. Blooms fall and fly.

Disposables

Around the big galleries I'll walk
and look and just take notes. Nothing to
record the occasion or weather
or politics or anything of
why be there.
                    Just e.g. the bird dead
and hanging upside down perfectly
believable. Three dimensional
wounds. Blood, red, carmine, yellow, the blues
of dead flesh. It would be hard to think
it, or just to do anything, but list
the supposed palette. Splat. Renaissance
chemicals – I've heard expressed the cost
price of reproduction. So think, no
record. I'm so not in the picture.
A harsh day in another notebook.
This is as plain as you fancy. Trash.
Rule off. Neat. Go next door to the next
application, next disposables.
The most ego-defining inkwells.

How it was, to be in another
exhibition. For what's not shaming
or to be ashamed of. That's where the
torture is allowed and framed, guarded
for ever, for me so tactfully.

Tears

Oh tears. Would this have been?
Claim that as assertion. Claim
it as clean flesh frightening from the rock.

Better in the imagination than.
Suck it as sea like local
granite. Like bent old toe-

nails surviving till ex-
humation. Come back, come back,
come back to make worth the truth of telling.

It's still spoken or written in the words
or the facts or the events
or anywhere. Earth – sick

it up. Vomit your best
tearful beauty till it dies
back for more tries, trials or tooth extractions.

Cut-Out

Close your eyes and look down as though from
high above a road, from when it's
azure blue, as a country

track it's silent, inexpressive,
and, though waiting for earth's fall,
and array of gravity's choices

for the colours, you see as
you fall, to end in a nice colour-
scheme that microsecond beneath

the map, cartridge paper or tracing
or cut-out or join-the-dots or
folded and creased precisely.

To the end, it would have stayed gentle
and very cold and now closely black.

Silence

Music, the other day, was
as complex as that home silence
after walking hard in the wind and

stopping to listen to something so
close that history almost
came in to circulate, thumping

oxygen to be consumed in
red cells, political commitment,
a short moment's colourful

estrangement to be sure of
itself, all fugues compressed to one
second's timespace, digest maths sweetly.

Nerve Fibres

I think of flying through isobars,
lines of even pressure, in a
plane, not knowing anything

of what's through that murky window
glass touch-cold and thinly spaced
and shuddering as the wind changes

precisely, to love wings' lift
and elevation through ice and night
in the same unforceable tracks

the nerve fibres use with spinal clouds
of fat and calcium to touch
landfall, pleasure, finger tips.

Note

Sleeping Sickness, Narcolepsy and the 'Narcolepsy' sequence of poems

I was born in Sheffield and my mother studied medicine at the University of Sheffield from about 1918 to 1922 or '23. She didn't qualify as a doctor because of her own repeated illnesses but graduated with a BSc in Physiology, I think, and worked for some years in the University Pathology Lab. Amongst those she worked with, or for, was the Professor of Pathology, Howard Florey, who later turned Alexander Fleming's discovery into usable penicillin and shared the Nobel Prize with him. During the war, Sheffield was badly bombed. My father went on working as a teacher until his school was hit. I think my mother went on in the Path. Lab.

She left work after the war, and when we moved to London in 1947 she took her microscope with her. I do not recall in any detail what her work had been, and whether it was simply the technical business of producing and processing samples or whether she was more deeply involved with research. However, to the best of my recollection she told me that the anatomical sections that she took from human brains and spinal cords were used for research into the many cases of sleeping sickness or narcolepsy (which words?) after the First World War. Strangely, among the earliest material I looked at through a microscope when I was myself a child, were some of those very slides, by then very old. I can still see the stained slivers of flesh and her neat writing on each label.